MEET THE GREATS

Florence NIGHTINGALE

TIM COOKE

Gareth Stevens
PUBLISHING

Please visit our website, **www.garethstevens.com**.
For a free color catalog of all our high-quality books,
call toll free 1-800-542-2595 or fax 1-877-542-2596.

CATALOGING-IN-PUBLICATION DATA

Names: Cooke, Tim.
Title: Florence Nightingale / Tim Cooke.
Description: New York : Gareth Stevens, 2017. | Series: Meet the greats | Includes index.
Identifiers: ISBN 9781482459487 (pbk.) | ISBN 9781482459500 (library bound) | ISBN 9781482459494 (6 pack)
Subjects: LCSH: Nightingale, Florence, 1820-1910--Juvenile literature. | Nurses--Great Britain--Biography.
Classification: LCC RT37.N5 C66 2017 | DDC 610.73--dc23

Published in 2017 by
Gareth Stevens Publishing
111 East 14th Street, Suite 349
New York, NY 10003

Copyright © 2017 Brown Bear Books Ltd

For Brown Bear Books Ltd:
Editorial Director: Lindsey Lowe
Managing Editor: Tim Cooke
Children's Publisher: Anne O'Daly
Design Manager: Keith Davis
Designer and illustrator: Supriya Sahai
Picture Manager: Sophie Mortimer

Concept development: Square and Circus / Brown Bear Books Ltd

Picture Credits: Front Cover: Character artwork, Supriya Sahai. Interior: All photographs courtesy Wellcome Foundation Images except, Library of Congress: 14b, 19, 21, 22, 35, 41; Shutterstock: Tewan Banditnukkanka 15b, Johanna Goodyear 18b, Romas Photos 8; Thinkstock: istockphoto 9, 18t, 24, 31; Wikipedia: Bassano 30, Simon Harriyott 34, Oosoom 43.

Character artwork © Supriya Sahai
All other artworks Brown Bear Books Ltd

Printed in China
CPSIA compliance information: Batch CW17GS: For further information contact Gareth Stevens, New York, New York at 1-800-542-2595.

Contents

Introduction

After Queen Victoria, Florence Nightingale was the most famous British woman of the 19th century.

Born into a rich family, Florence was expected to marry a rich man, have a family and lead a quiet life. But Florence had no intention of becoming a wife and mother. From a young age, she wanted to help the sick.

Florence's desire to help others changed the way we live. She was the founder of modern nursing. Before Florence, nurses were untrained, but she saw that nursing had to become a **profession**. She went to run a hospital during the Crimean War (1853–1856). Because she carried a lamp at night, the patients called her "The Lady with the Lamp." Florence asked the British government to improve hospitals. She was one of the first people to link disease and poor **hygiene**.

Florence never did marry. Instead, she dedicated her long life to improving the lives of others.

A Young NURSE

Florence Nightingale was born into great wealth and privilege. But at age 16 she turned her back on her life of luxury.

Florence Nightingale was born on May 12, 1820. Her father, William Nightingale, had inherited land and a lead mine from his father, who had been a rich banker. William did not need to earn money. Instead he spent his time traveling and reading. He married Florence's mother, Fanny, in 1818 and the couple left England for a two-year honeymoon in Europe. Florence was named for Florence in Italy, the city where she was born. Her older sister, Parthenope, was also named after her birthplace. Parthenope was an old name for the Italian city of Naples.

QUICK FACTS

* Florence's family was so rich she didn't have to work!

* Florence believed she heard God telling her to help other people.

The city of Florence in Italy.

A PRIVILEGED CHILDHOOD

When Florence was one year old, the Nightingale family returned to England. The girls and their parents divided their time between their two main family homes in the English countryside. They also made long trips to London for social events. They had lots of servants to look after them everywhere they went. Because the name Parthenope was long and difficult to pronounce, everyone called Florence's elder sister "Parthe."

A SERIOUS EDUCATION

As was normal for girls in wealthy families at that time, the Nightingale sisters were not sent to school. Instead, **governesses** taught them at home. Their mother, Fanny, taught them music, art, dancing, and needlework. She believed such skills would make Florence and her sister good wives and daughters. When Florence was 11, her father also began to teach his daughters. William loved math, literature, and history. Unlike her sister, Florence was an eager and smart student. She learned five languages, and she often discussed politics and business with her family. Parthe was much happier organizing grand parties with their mother.

Parthe Nightingale loved to organize parties.

A DIVINE CALL

On February 7, 1837, when Florence was age 16, she was walking in the grounds of the family home at Embley Park, Hampshire. She believed she heard God speak to her. He told her that he wanted her to serve him. At the time, she did not understand how she might do this, but it was already clear to her that her life must have a purpose. It was not going to be like the lives of other upper-class women like her sister.

In 1838, the Nightingales took the two girls on another long trip around Europe. Fanny wanted them to get ready for married life. In Europe, Florence visited hospitals in many cities. She also studied the work of **charities**. While in Paris she met Mary Clarke, who became her friend for forty years. Mary had some **radical** ideas for the time. She thought women were equal to men in everything.

The family home at Embley Park, Hampshire, England.

IDEAS OF NURSING

Returning to her comfortable life in Britain in 1839, Florence could see that most people were not as lucky as she was. She often visited sick and poor people who lived on her family's **estates** to help in whatever way she could. Perhaps, she began to think, God wanted her to become a nurse to help the sick.

However, when Florence suggested to her parents that she train as a nurse, they refused to allow it. In England in the 1840s, nurses held a very low social position. They had no special medical training and were regarded as little more than servants. Now age 25, Florence felt trapped. She could not do anything without her parents' permission. Her parents despaired when she turned down proposals from men who wanted to marry her.

A young Florence Nightingale.

OVERSEAS AGAIN

Hoping Florence might change her mind and get married, her parents allowed her to travel with some family friends to Italy, Egypt, and Greece. In Italy she met Sidney Herbert, who worked for the British government. They shared an interest in training women to be nurses and improving the dreadful Victorian hospitals.

On her trip, Florence also spent two weeks at the Kaiserswerth Institute in Germany in 1849. It was a religious community that also trained nurses, and Florence had by now decided to become a nurse. When she got home and her parents found out where she had been, they were furious.

Florence visited these ancient ruins in Egypt with her friends.

Sidney Herbert.

Parthe was so upset she became ill and Florence had to stay home and nurse her. This made Florence even more determined to become a nurse. Finally, her parents gave in. They told Florence she could return to Germany and train for three months at the Institute. She was overjoyed.

Back at the Kaiserswerth Institute in 1851, Florence learned how vital it was to train nurses in order to improve patient care and the way hospitals were run. At the end of her training, she knew she had to continue nursing. Her mother and sister were still unhappy that Florence wanted to work, but her father could now see how important it was to his daughter. He gave Florence a generous **allowance** that enabled her to become financially **independent**. Finally, Florence could leave home and do whatever she wanted.

Pastor Fliedner founded the Kaiserswerth Institute.

19th-Century MEDICINE

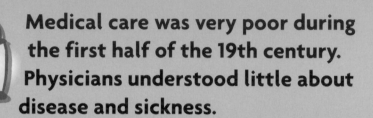

Medical care was very poor during the first half of the 19th century. Physicians understood little about disease and sickness.

Physicians believed disease was spread by bad air, called **miasmas**. The main role of a physician was to provide comfort to his patients. Surgery was performed without **anesthetic**, which was first used in 1846. Physicians were always men. The first female physician in America was Elizabeth Blackwell. In 1849, she graduated from medical school in New York City. She and Florence Nightingale later became friends.

Nursing did not exist as a profession. Nurses were usually old ladies who had no medical training. They had a reputation for drinking and ignoring their patients! Physicians treated them badly and they were poorly paid.

Physician Elizabeth Blackwell.

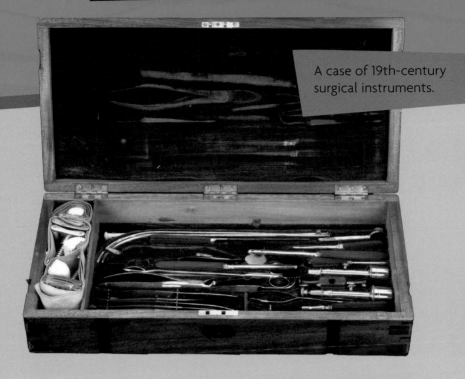

A case of 19th-century surgical instruments.

Hospitals tended to be dirty places. People did not understand the connection between hygiene and disease. No one yet knew that disease was spread by **germs**. Florence Nightingale was one of the first people to understand that dirt helped to spread infection. In city slums, disease spread easily and quickly because of cramped housing. The death rate among poor people was much higher than among wealthier people.

Even at the end of the 19th century, hospitals offered little medical care. Only the poor went to hospitals. Rich people were treated at home, where the physician visited them.

Germs seen under a microscope.

15

The CRIMEAN WAR

In 1854, Great Britain went to war with Russia far away in the Crimea, a place on the Black Sea near Turkey.

The war changed Florence's life forever. With the money from her father, Florence left the family home for London in 1853. She was now 33 years old. She got a job in charge of a nursing home for "gentlewomen" in Harley Street, London. Harley Street was the most famous street in London for physicians' offices.

Florence was not paid for her work in the nursing home. In Victorian times, very wealthy women did not take paid employment. It was considered to be beneath their social status. Florence did not care about earning money, however. She finally had the job she wanted.

QUICK FACTS

* About 21,000 British soldiers died in the Crimean War.
* Of them, about 16,000 died of disease rather than wounds from the battlefield!

Harley Street in London.

A HAPPY YEAR

Florence's training in Germany had taught her how to run the hospital efficiently. She had also learned some skills from watching how her father ran the family's estates. She knew how to save money by buying large amounts of medicine at the same time. She insisted that the hospital be cleaned and the bed linen washed and changed regularly. She made sure the staff served healthy food to the patients. She trained the nurses to look after the patients' needs. At the end of the year, however, Florence felt she had improved the hospital as much as she could. She started to look for a new position.

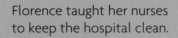

Florence taught her nurses to keep the hospital clean.

THE WAR BEGINS

In March 1854, British newspapers started to report from the Crimean **Peninsula**, where British, French, and Turkish forces were fighting the Russians. The reports said that wounded British soldiers were suffering terrible conditions. They were dying from disease. They had very little medicine or food.

Florence's friend, Sidney Herbert, was now the Secretary at War in the British government. It was his job to provide care for wounded and sick soldiers. He decided to ask Florence to travel to the Crimea with some female nurses to take care of the soldiers. He wrote to Florence saying, "There is but one person in England that I know of who would be capable of organizing … such a scheme."

British troops go into battle against the Russians.

Florence, meanwhile, had just written to Sidney with her own idea: that she should go to the Crimea with some nurses. Their letters crossed in the mail! Florence accepted Sidney's offer. Within a week, she had selected the nurses to go with her, had uniforms made, and had assembled medical supplies.

In October 1854, Florence and thirty-nine nurses left England for the military hospital at Scutari in Turkey. The British newspapers described Florence as a heroine. They reported every day on her progress toward the Crimea. The British public were amazed and impressed that a woman of Florence's background would travel thousands of miles to look after wounded soldiers. When *The Times* newspaper asked for **donations** to help Florence, money and supplies flooded in.

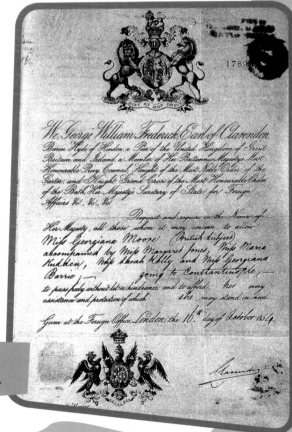

A passport that allowed Florence's nurses to travel.

The Barrack Hospital at Scutari.

A SHOCKING ARRIVAL

The nurses sailed from Marseilles in the south of France on October 27, 1854. They crossed the Mediterranean Sea and arrived in what is now Istanbul in Turkey. Then they crossed the Bosphorus Strait to Scutari, where wounded British soldiers were cared for at hospitals including the Barrack Hospital.

Conditions were far worse than Florence had expected. To get to the hospital from the battlefields, wounded soldiers had been carried more than 300 miles (480 km) by ship across the Black Sea. There was little medical care onboard the ships. Many of the men arrived at Scutari with serious diseases such as **cholera**, **dysentery**, and **typhus**.

TERRIBLE CONDITIONS

Once the soldiers arrived at Scutari, there were not enough beds to go around. Many men slept on the filthy floors. Rats, lice, and fleas were everywhere. The smell was terrible. Beneath the hospitals lay blocked **sewers**. There was little fresh water, **chamber pots** overflowed, and the food was terrible. Soldiers ate moldy green bread and meat that was as tough as shoe leather.

After Florence's initial shock, things got worse. The military physicians were not happy to have female nurses in their hospitals. To start with, they simply refused to let Florence and her nurses take care of the wounded soldiers.

Then, a few days after Florence arrived, 500 more wounded soldiers arrived from the battlefields. At least another thousand were also on their way. The physicians realized that they needed all the help they could get. They reluctantly allowed Florence and her nurses to go to work in the Barrack Hospital.

Florence immediately ordered her nurses to clean the hospital throughout. She rented a nearby house where they could wash bed linen, and she ordered the chamber pots to be emptied often. She also got her nurses to sew mattresses and stuff them with fresh straw. That way, soldiers did not have to lie on the floor. Things soon started to improve.

Florence was shocked by conditions in the hospital.

The Hospital at SCUTARI

Soon after arriving in Scutari, Florence introduced many practices that are still used in hospitals today.

Florence understood how important it was that sick people should eat healthy food. She ordered her nurses to prepare good meals using fresh vegetables. She also knew that wounds must be kept clean and dressings changed frequently. She bought fabric to make bandages, clothes, and pillows to make the patients more comfortable.

When the hospital's own supplies ran out, Florence used the supplies she had brought to Turkey from England.

Florence carried an oil lamp at night.

Florence patrols the wards in the hospital.

Although the physicians did not like Florence and her colleagues, the soldiers all loved the nurses. Florence worked 20 hours a day. At night, she walked up and down the long hallways lined with beds. She carried an oil lamp, so the soldiers called her the "Lady with the Lamp."

Despite all the improvements, the death rate at the Barrack Hospital remained high. More soldiers died there than in the hospitals closer to the battlefront. Then an investigation discovered that gases from the blocked sewers beneath the hospital were poisoning the soldiers. When the drains were cleaned, the death rate dropped almost overnight.

National
FAME

Florence fell sick in 1855 while visiting other hospitals in the Crimea. The British public held their breath, waiting for their heroine to recover.

*I*n May 1855 Florence sailed across the Black Sea to visit British hospitals in the Crimea itself. She fell sick with a fever that left her weak and unable to work until the end of the summer. When she recovered, Florence returned to the Barrack Hospital. She was even more determined to improve the quality of life for the wounded soldiers. She set up reading rooms and provided activities to keep the men occupied as they began their recovery. She also persuaded many men to send their pay home instead of wasting it on gambling and drinking.

QUICK FACTS
* When Florence arrived home after the war, she was famous!
* The public gave money to a fund to allow her to continue her work improving hospitals.

WELL LOVED

The soldiers adored Florence. She treated them respectfully and with understanding, which was unusual for the time. Most soldiers were from the lower social classes. They were often treated badly by their officers and by the military physicians. But Florence never seemed to be too busy to sit with a sick soldier. She wrote letters home for soldiers who did not know how to write, and read them letters they received. If a soldier died, she wrote to his family because she knew that they would want to be told about their sons, husbands, or fathers.

Florence wrote letters for soldiers who could not write.

The Crimean War ended with the signing of the Treaty of Paris on March 30, 1856. Florence stayed at Scutari nursing the sick until July. Then she sailed for home. She was now 36 years old.

A HEROINE

Unknown to her, in her absence, Florence had become a national heroine. Not only were baby girls being named "Florence" in her honor, but there were also ships and racehorses called Florence. Her admirers wrote poems and stories about her. The Sultan of Turkey sent her a diamond bracelet in thanks for her work, and Queen Victoria wrote her a letter of thanks.

Florence hated all the fuss. When she took the train home to her family, she traveled under the name of "Miss Smith" to avoid drawing attention to herself. Her family, however, was excited about Florence's fame. They wanted her to attend all the parties held in her honor and to speak at public meetings. But Florence was worn out. She just wanted to rest. More importantly, she also wanted to continue her work of improving hospitals and public health. She was still angry with herself for allowing so many men to die at Scutari before she had found out about the poisonous gases.

A NEW MISSION

Florence did accept one invitation. She went to meet Queen Victoria and her husband, Prince Albert, at Balmoral Castle, their home in Scotland. Florence told the queen what was wrong with the military hospitals and what needed to be done to improve them.

Queen Victoria appreciated Florence's work.

Kensington Palace in London.

Queen Victoria asked Florence to organize whatever improvements were necessary. She was very impressed by Florence and wrote, "Such a head! I wish we had her at the War Office." Later, Queen Victoria offered Florence her own apartment in Kensington Palace, one of the royal residences in London. Florence turned down the offer. She did not want any special treatment.

THE NIGHTINGALE FUND

Many people wanted to show their appreciation of Florence's achievements in the Crimea. Many of them gave money to the Nightingale Fund. The fund was set up to raise money to allow Florence to continue with her nursing reforms.

Florence wanted to apply the knowledge she had gained from two years in the military hospitals to hospitals in Britain. While she was at home, still recovering from the fever she had caught in the Crimea, Florence spent hours working in her bed. She put together lots of **statistics**. Of the 18,000 men who died, Florence worked out that 16,000 had died from preventable diseases rather than from battlefield wounds. She wanted to make sure that, in the future, the lives of soldiers would not be put at risk through a lack of hygiene.

Florence working at home after the end of the war.

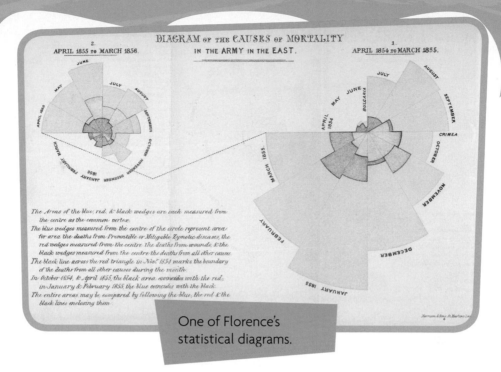

One of Florence's statistical diagrams.

Florence wrote hundreds of letters to important people explaining her findings. She persuaded her friends in the government to set up a **Royal Commission** to study the health of the army. The Commission agreed to a number of improvements that saved many lives in the future. The Army started to train its physicians better. It also made sure that its hospitals were cleaner, with better food and proper clothes for patients to wear. But Florence was far from finished.

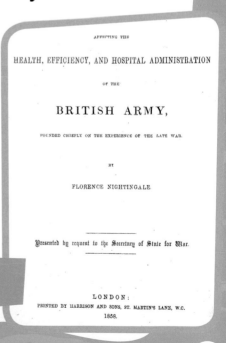

Florence's report on the Crimean War.

Mary SEACOLE

Known as "Mother Seacole" to the soldiers she nursed in the Crimean War, Mary Seacole's story is just as remarkable as that of Florence Nightingale.

Mary was born in Jamaica in 1805. At the time, Jamaica was part of the British Empire. Mary worked from an early age. She and her mother ran a hotel where wounded British soldiers came to rest.

When the Crimean War broke out, Jamaican soldiers enlisted to fight in the British Army. Mary decided that she would travel to the Crimea as well to offer her services. She arrived in London three days before Florence left with her first group of nurses. Mary tried to join a second group of Florence's nurses but was unsuccessful.

GREATER LONDON COUNCIL
MARY SEACOLE
1805~1881
Jamaican Nurse
HEROINE OF THE CRIMEAN WAR
lived here

A plaque in London marks Seacole's home.

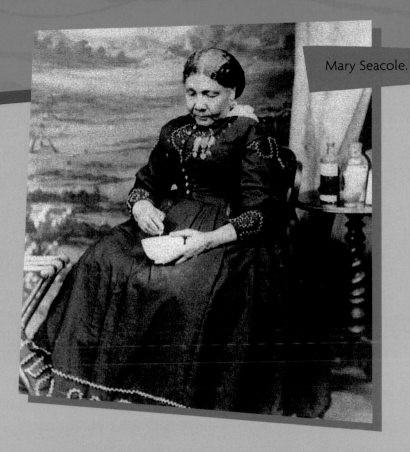

Mary Seacole.

Instead Seacole funded her own trip. She sailed for the Crimea in January 1855 with supplies and medicines. She set up the British Hotel close to Balaclava in the Crimea, where the British were fighting. Mary sold the soldiers healthy food, warm clothes, and blankets (in those days soldiers had to buy all their own supplies).

Mary nursed sick soldiers back to health at her hotel. When the war finished, she returned to London. The soldiers wrote letters praising Mary's work in the Crimea and she soon became famous for helping soldiers. Oddly enough, Mary and Florence only ever met once in the Crimea—for just five minutes.

A Medical
REFORMER

Florence's health never recovered fully from the fever she caught in the Crimea, but she did not allow poor health to stop her life's work.

*F*lorence spent much of the last 40 years of her life in bed because of her poor health. But she was not sleeping—she was still hard at work! In 1859 she wrote her most famous books, *Notes on Hospitals* and *Notes on Nursing*. In the books, Florence set out her ideas of how to improve nursing both at home and in hospitals. The next year, she opened her own nursing school.

NOTES ON HOSPITALS:

BEING

TWO PAPERS READ BEFORE THE NATIONAL ASSOCIATION
FOR THE PROMOTION OF SOCIAL SCIENCE,
AT LIVERPOOL, IN OCTOBER, 1858.

WITH

EVIDENCE GIVEN TO THE ROYAL COMMISSIONERS
ON THE STATE OF THE ARMY IN 1857.

BY

FLORENCE NIGHTINGALE.

LONDON:
JOHN W. PARKER AND SON, WEST STRAND.
1859.

Florence Nightingale's book *Notes on Hospitals*.

QUICK FACTS

* Florence spent the last decades of her life in bed!
* She wrote thousands of letters to encourage reform of medical care.

THE NIGHTINGALE TRAINING SCHOOL

The Nightingale Home and Training School for Nurses opened in London in July 1860. Training lasted for a year, and every nurse wore a plain brown uniform with a **starched** white apron and hat. Florence was very proud of her nurses. When they completed their training, she would invite them for tea at her home in order to meet them. The Nightingale method of teaching was very successful. It soon spread across England and as far as Australia, America, and Africa. The school was the first to teach women about general nursing and **midwifery** as a formal profession according to Florence's beliefs.

Florence and a group of Nightingale Nurses.

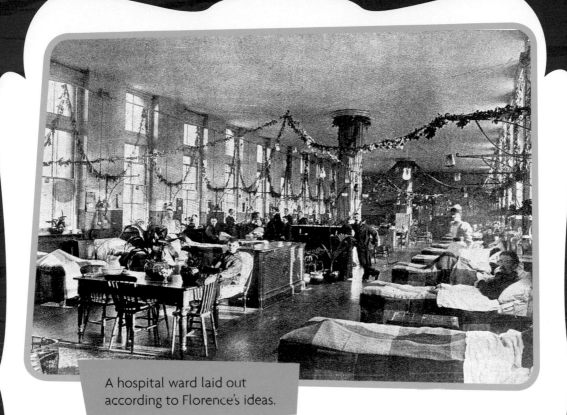

A hospital ward laid out according to Florence's ideas.

From her experiences in the Crimea, Florence knew that disease spread when patients were kept in dirty, cramped conditions. She believed that better **ventilation** and better **sanitation** were vital. That meant keeping hospitals clean and well aired. She also believed that patients had a better chance of recovery if they were in rooms with natural sunlight and windows that opened. Over the next few decades, other health professionals came to see that Florence was right.

NEW RESEARCH

From her bed, Florence continued to think up new ways of improving public health—even on the other side of the world. India was then part of the British Empire. Florence noted that British soldiers in India seemed to have a high death rate. India also had a large population of mainly poor, uneducated people, many of whom died young from disease and hunger. Florence wrote to physicians in India, asking them about the sort of sicknesses that killed not just soldiers but also the people. When Florence included all the information in a report it was 2,000 pages long!

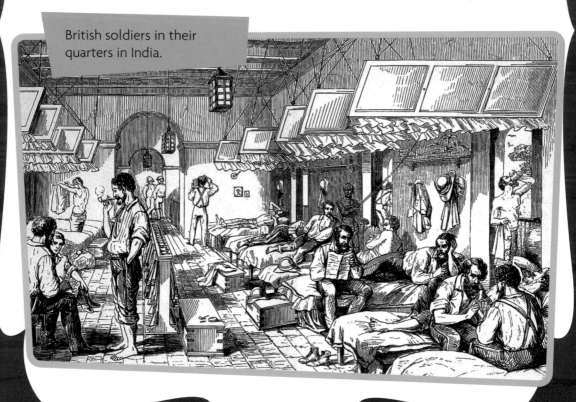

British soldiers in their quarters in India.

It was clear that people and soldiers in India suffered from the same problems she had seen in the Crimea: bad drainage, bad sanitation, a lack of fresh air, dirty water, and overcrowding. Few people had

Wounded soldiers and their nurses in the US Civil War.

their own freshwater supply or bathrooms, and few Indians understood the connection between good health and good sanitation. Florence knew that to improve the army's living conditions, she also had to campaign to improve conditions for ordinary Indians. She continued to receive reports from India until 1906.

THE CIVIL WAR

During the American Civil War (1861–1865), both the Union and the Confederate sides wrote to Florence Nightingale to ask her advice on how to improve their military medical services. She was happy to write reports for both sides. She did not want any soldiers to die unnecessarily.

KEEPING BUSY

At home, Florence nursed both her parents through their last illnesses. It was not until she was 60 years old that she was free of her duties to care for her family. She spent the remainder of her life keeping busy, even though she continued to suffer from a disease called chronic brucellosis, which had caused the fever she had caught in the Crimea. She suffered badly from depression and was often in terrible pain. She wrote around 13,000 letters as part of her health campaigns. For over 30 years she corresponded regularly with Queen Victoria. The queen adopted many of Florence's ideas. Over Victoria's long reign, from 1837 to 1901, public health in Britain steadily improved.

Florence Nightingale working in bed in her old age.

RECOGNITION

Florence remained a private and modest person. She believed she was carrying out the work God had asked her to do all those years earlier. But many people wanted to recognize Florence's **dedication** to improving people's lives. In 1907, when Florence was 87 years old, King Edward VIII (Queen Victoria's son) awarded her the Order of Merit. This is the highest **honor** given in Great Britain. Florence Nightingale was the first woman to receive the order. She is supposed to have said, "Too kind, too kind," when the medal was given to her.

Florence Nightingale died on August 13, 1910. She had asked for her body to be used for medical research, but instead the **authorities** wanted to give her a proper funeral. She was buried next to her parents near her childhood home. Soldiers whose units had fought in the Crimean War carried her coffin. She was 90 and had outlived almost everyone she had known in her younger days.

Timeline

1820   · Born in Florence, Italy.

1837   · Queen Victoria comes to the throne. Florence believes God speaks to her.

1838   · On another tour of Europe, Florence meets her friend Mary Clarke in Paris.

1842   · Florence finds out about the nurses' hospital in Kaiserswerth in Germany.

1844   · Florence begins visiting hospitals in Britain and abroad.

1849   · Florence sets out on a trip to Italy, Egypt, and Greece. On her way home, she visits the Kaiserswerth Institute in Germany.

1851   · Florence spends three months studying nursing in Kaiserswerth.

1853   · Florence becomes Superintendent of the Institute for the Care of Sick Gentlewomen in London.

1854   · Florence recruits nurses to travel to the Crimea, where British soldiers are fighting a war.
        · *The Times* newspaper raises money to buy medical supplies for Florence.
        · Florence and her nurses travel to Scutari in Turkey.
        · Florence reforms the military hospitals in Scutari.

1855   · Florence visits military hospitals near the battlefields.
        · Florence becomes very sick with a fever.

1856	· Florence is welcomed as a heroine when she returns to Britain after the war.
	· Florence is invited to meet Queen Victoria for the first time.
1857	· Florence is made a member of a Royal Commission on army health.
1859	· *Notes on Nursing* and *Notes on Hospitals* are published.
1860	· The Nightingale Home and Training School for Nurses opens in London.
1861	· The American Civil War begins. Florence advises both sides about care for sick and wounded soldiers.
1867	· Florence advises on the improvement of nursing in hospitals for the poor.
1901	· Queen Victoria dies.
1907	· Florence is awarded the Order of Merit.
1910	· Florence dies on August 13, in London.

KEY PUBLICATIONS

✤ *Notes on Matters Affecting the Health, Efficiency, and Hospital Administration of the British Army* (1858)

✤ *Notes on Hospitals* (1859)

✤ *Notes on Nursing: What It Is, and What It Is Not* (1860)

✤ *Observations on the Evidence Contained in the Stational Reports submitted to the Royal Commission on the Sanitary State of the Army in India* (1863)

✤ *On Trained Nurses for the Sick Poor* (1876)

Glossary

allowance A regular gift of money for someone to live off.

anesthetic A substance that reduces pain.

authorities Representatives of the government.

chamber pots Bowls used to go to the bathroom.

charities Organizations that raise money for people in need.

cholera A serious disease caused by drinking dirty water.

dedication Commitment to a task.

donations Sums of money given to a charity.

dysentery An infection of the intestines that causes diarrhea.

estates Privately owned parcels of land.

germs Tiny organisms that spread disease.

governesses Women employed to educate children at home.

honor An official award.

hygiene Practices that prevent disease, such as keeping clean.

independent Able to make decisions for oneself.

miasmas Unhealthy fumes.

midwifery The practice of assisting at the birth of a baby.

peninsula A piece of land that sticks out into a body of water.

profession A paid occupation with long training and a formal qualification.

radical Extreme.

Royal Commission An official group that holds an inquiry on behalf of the government.

sanitation The process of keeping places clean.

sewers Pipes that carry waste water.

starched Stiffened with starch.

statistics Numerical data.

typhus An infectious fever spread by lice, insects, and fleas.

ventilation The circulation of fresh air in a room.

Further Resources

Books

Aller, Susan Bivin. *Florence Nightingale.* History Makers. Minneapolis: Lerner Publications, 2009.

Gorrell, Gena K. *Heart and Soul: The Story of Florence Nightingale.* Toronto: Tundra Books, 2005.

Hinman, Bonnie. *Florence Nightingale and the Advancement of Nursing.* Uncharted, Unexplored, and Unexplained. Hockessin, Del.: Mitchell Lane Publishers, 2014.

Robbins, Tina, and Anne Timmons. *Florence Nightingale: Lady with the Lamp.* Graphic Biographies. New York: Capstone Press, 2007.

Websites

BBC History
www.bbc.co.uk/schools/ primaryhistory/famouspeople/ florence_nightingale/
A biography and timeline of Florence's life, with links to images and videos.

Florence Nightingale Museum
www.florence-nightingale.co.uk/
Click on "The Collection" for links to Florence's biography and other resources.

History.com
www.history.com/topics/ womens-history/florence -nightingale
A biography of Florence's career with videos and other links.

Spartacus Educational
spartacus-educational.com/ REnightingale.htm
A biography of Florence and her influence on nursing.

Index